SEA OF TERROR

BY SAM CATLIN

SEA OF TERROR premiered at the Hudson Theatre Mainstage, Los Angeles, on July 27, 2023, produced by Joanna Colbert and Julie Dretzin. It was directed by Sam Catlin, the lighting design was by Steve Pope, the sound design was by Alysha Grace Bermudez, and the stage manager was Ellora Venkat. The cast was as follows:

ALICE .... Julie Dretzin
BEN .... John Ales
DANNY .... Paul Schulze
DORIS .... Amy Scribner

CHARACTERS

ALICE

BEN

DANNY

DORIS

SEA OF TERROR

SCENE ONE

"Scary music" comes in as—

The lights come halfway up on the living room of a modest, suburban home.

An upstage center door leads into the kitchen. A stage left door leads to a hallway. A stage right door leads to a bedroom. There is also a window downstage right.

Downstage, two couches are set around a coffee table.

Ben, a man wearing khakis, a dress shirt, and clean sneakers, half lies/lounges on a couch watching an offstage TV.

After a moment, Alice enters wearing a little sweater over a pretty dress and holding a tray of cocktail snacks.

She comes and goes arranging the snacks on the table.

At one point, Ben rises and crosses to the downstage "window" and looks out.

After several beats of Alice setting up, the lights come up full, the music cuts out, and—

ALICE. Ready?

Ben doesn't respond.

After a moment of consideration...Alice rearranges the snacks into a different configuration.

Satisfied, she turns and heads back upstage.

(*As she exits.*) Your jacket's hanging on the thing.

Alice exits.

(*Offstage.*) Honey?

Ben doesn't respond.

(Offstage.) Hon?

> *Ben doesn't respond.*

(Offstage.) Honey?

> *Ben rolls his eyes, stands, and exits stage right.*
>
> *Ben reenters, putting on a sport coat. He returns to his spot on the couch. He takes a moment to consider the spread that Alice has laid out on the table before he resumes watching TV. Alice reenters and pauses upstage, uneasy.*

I've lost the Christopher Cross CD.

> *Beat.*

Baby? I can't find the Christopher Cross.

BEN. No?

ALICE. I know; I thought it would be nice.

BEN. It would be nice.

ALICE. *(Noticing him.)* What's wrong?

BEN. Nothing.

> *Alice considers her husband a moment before deciding to reach out with some "interested" conversation—*

ALICE. *(Referring to the TV.)* What's that?

BEN. The John Deere Senior Classic.

> *She watches.*

ALICE. Is that golf?

BEN. Yes.

> *She watches.*

ALICE. Where's that man walking?

BEN. He's walking to hit his ball.

> *She watches.*

ALICE. Again?

BEN. *(Snaps.)* Yes.

ALICE. What's wrong?

BEN. Nothing. You're just—you're talking a lot.

ALICE. And you're not.

BEN. Okay, so?

ALICE. So nothing. *(Then.)* So fine.

> *Alice rises, crosses to the window, and "pulls back" the curtain. She stands looking out for a long moment. Ben sits up.*

BEN. What?

ALICE. I thought I heard a car door. *(Releasing the curtain.)* Not yet. *(Turns to exit.)* Soon though.

> *Alice exits.*

> *Ben stands and goes to look out the window himself.*

> *As he looks outside we begin to build in sounds of an "outside world." Cars honking, children playing, planes flying overhead, the din of a crowd, etc. The sounds begin to build and seem about to turn into something almost sinister, when—*

(Offstage.) Oh no!

BEN. *(Startled.)* What?! What happened?

> *Alice reenters.*

ALICE. I think I've lost it.

BEN. You haven't lost it.

ALICE. Well, I don't know where it went.

BEN. Alright, so, okay.

> *Ben keeps his cool and tries to problem solve.*

If you can't find the, uh…?

ALICE. Christopher Cross.

BEN. …CD. Then how about some other one?

ALICE. Like what?

BEN. Like anything. Ambrosia? Gordon Lightfoot? How about the guy with the—that guy who started wearing those weird dresses?

ALICE. …Cat Stevens?

BEN. Right? So good with the…

> *A moment as Ben attempts to hum a song he doesn't know from an artist he can't remember.*

ALICE. *(Brightening a little.)* You think so?

BEN. *(His most reassuring.)* I really do.

> *Small beat.*

ALICE. *(Frowns.)* I can't believe I lost the Christopher Cross.

BEN. *(Snaps suddenly.)* Well you did, Alice! You did! You lost it! It's gone, there's nothing we can do, so just, you need to just…

> *Ben can't think of how to complete the thought so he returns to the couch.*

ALICE. I thought you were going to try and not get so nervous tonight?

BEN. I'm not nervous. *("What about you?")* I'm nervous?

> *Alice sits on the couch.*

ALICE. Sweetheart we talked about this, remember? People are coming over for a drink and I love you. That's it. That's the beginning and the end of the big scary thing. Okay?

BEN. I said I'm not nervous.

ALICE. Good.

BEN. But it's not so crazy of me to have certain apprehensions.

ALICE. Did I just say that you were crazy?

BEN. No.

ALICE. Did you just say that I was crazy?

BEN. N-no.

ALICE. Has anyone ever said to anyone else that they were crazy?

BEN. *(A bit confused.)* W-what—?

ALICE. *(Overlap, with optimism.)* Life is a relentless sea of terror and peril. But you and I see this storm and are throwing up a brave sail. And tonight we're going to see what foreign beach we're thrown upon. *(Then.)* I am so proud of us.

BEN. I swear to gosh: if he starts teasing me about my hair.

ALICE. I know.

BEN. I will put my foot down *so* fast.

ALICE. Great! You should! You would have every right. *(Then.)* Although, I think it'll be fine. No one wants a repeat of last time.

> *Alice glances uneasily at the TV.*

You'll turn that off soon.

> *She stands and moves to exit upstage center.*

(Noticing.) That blazer looks wonderful on you, are those the penny loafers we bought you?

   Ben shrugs.

Ben.

BEN. They don't fit.

ALICE. They don't fit?

BEN. The heels are tight.

ALICE. Now, hold on a minute: Your brand-new English Manners penny loafers that we just spent one hundred and twenty-five dollars on at Florsheim don't fit? The "heels are tight" so you're not wearing them? *(Then.)* This is news to me.

BEN. Well, now you're all caught up.

ALICE. *(Threatening.)* I'd put those shoes on if I were you.

BEN. No.

ALICE. I'd put those shoes on if I were you.

BEN. No.

ALICE. Go put on those shoes.

BEN. No.

ALICE. Go put those shoes on.

BEN. *No.*

ALICE. They're coming over.

BEN. So?

ALICE. "So?" She'll see you. She'll see you in those sneakers.

BEN. So?

ALICE. So she won't like them. She won't like them one bit.

BEN. She's not going to care.

ALICE. Oh, she'll care. Don't you worry about that. She'll care plenty.

BEN. What's that supposed to mean?

ALICE. It means *watch out. (Pleading.)* Don't you want to make an impression?

BEN. I'll make an impression!

ALICE. In those itty-bitty little gym jumpers? How are you going to make an impression?

BEN. I'll put my foot down, okay? I'll put my foot down and make an impression with my foot, if I have to. *(Had enough.)* Now, that's it about the shoes! End of discussion. You're just, you're being really weird and paranoid, Alice.

ALICE. I hope so.

> *Alice looks out the downstage window.*

I hope I'm not right about anything I'm thinking.

BEN. I'm telling you. The loafers don't matter. They're just dropping by. We'll sit down and talk for an hour or so and then they'll go and leave us alone.

> *She joins him on the couch.*

ALICE. I don't know.

BEN. We'll be fine. We'll "rise to the occasion," right? Isn't that what you always say?

ALICE. I'm sorry. I have a tendency to get caught up in the…

BEN. I know.

ALICE. I want everything to be, just exactly…

BEN. I know.

ALICE. But sometimes it isn't and that's life so get over it.

BEN. Exactly.

> *Ben double checks to make sure she's off this topic before he turns the TV back on.*
>
> *Alice's attention slowly drifts back to the sneakers.*

ALICE. I can't believe those shoes don't fit.

BEN. I know. The heels were a little pinchy.

ALICE. *(Sympathetic.)* Aw. Why didn't you say something?

BEN. I did say something.

ALICE. When?

BEN. At the store.

ALICE. You did?

BEN. Yeah.

ALICE. At the shoe store?

BEN. Yeah.

ALICE. That the heels were?

BEN. So pinchy. Like a fist with razors.

ALICE. Sweetheart.

Again, her attention slowly returns to his sneakers.

You never said those shoes—

BEN. *(Overlapping.)* Yes, I did!

ALICE. When?!

BEN. *(Repeats.) At the store.*
(Then.) I was sitting on the bench by the mirror next to the pole. You were standing by the rack with those hiking sneakers that you kept saying you liked. I put the loafers on and you said how much you liked the cable stitching on the sides and you asked me what I thought about the tassels, and I said I liked them fine.
(To be clear.) I said I liked the *tassels* fine, Alice.
(Then.) But when I stood up and walked around in them for a while and the salesman guy asked me how they felt, I said, "They're a little tight in the heel. The heels are a little tight." They were so uncomfortable, I actually began to consider the very real possibility of moving up to size elevens. But then, all of a sudden, that lady started screaming at her son because his feet stank and we got distracted when all hell started to break loose.

ALICE. You mean when you got nervous about those little children?

BEN. *(Defensive.)* I didn't get "nervous." And they weren't "little children," Alice. They were wilding teenagers. Crowding around, watching the lady yell, thinking it was so funny. I had no idea what was going to happen next. I was concerned for you and lost track of the loafers in all the confusion.

ALICE. You waited in the car while I put the shoes on my credit card.

BEN. Alice, I am seriously warning you to stop talking about my shoes.

ALICE. You never said anything about the heels being—

BEN. *(Talking over her.)* Alice, I am seriously warning you—

ALICE. I'm seriously warning YOU!

BEN. Alice, I swear to god: if you don't stop talking about those penny loafers, I am really going to not like it.

ALICE. *(Mocking.)* You're "really going to not like it"?

BEN. *(Warning.)* Alice.

ALICE. *(Mimicking.)* Ben.

BEN. *(Another warning.)* Alice.

ALICE. *(Mimicking.)* Ben.

BEN. *(A really big warning.)* ALICE.

> *She stands to leave.*

ALICE. *(Disgusted.)* Ugh, give me a break.

> *Ben stands too.*

BEN. I will give you a bad break if you're not careful.

ALICE. No you won't. You know why, Ben? Because you never do anything.

> *Alice exits upstage right. Ben's head starts to bob, and then, softly like a lullaby to himself, he sings a few lyrics from a hip-hop song like LL Cool J's "Mama Said Knock You Out."**
>
> *Ben goes to the downstage right window. And again those "outside" sounds begins to play. But only a short moment before the moment is interrupted as—*
>
> *Alice reenters.*

I so hope they like the cheese poppers.

> *Alice crosses and exits into the kitchen.*
>
> *Ben finds his way back to the couch.*
>
> *Alice reenters.*
>
> *She crosses downstage and sits on the arm of the couch.*
>
> *She watches.*

(Referring to the TV.) What's this?

BEN. *(sulking.) Today's Canadian Castles.*

ALICE. Ben: I'm sorry.

> *Ben doesn't respond.*

I'm sorry I said you don't do anything.

> *Ben doesn't respond.*

Ben—

BEN. I'm wearing my sneakers.

ALICE. Sweetheart, you can wear whatever you want.

BEN. I'm wearing these.

ALICE. Fine. *(Then.)* Great.

> *Alice turns away, checks herself in the stage right mirror.*

BEN. *(Mutters pointedly.)* Sorry we all can't look as good as you.

ALICE. *(Wheels around.)* What did you just say?

BEN. I said, "Sorry we all can't—"

ALICE. I heard you. *(Self-conscious, defensive.)* This is a sweater and a dress, Ben. A dress and a sweater.

BEN. Fine.

ALICE. If you've got something on your mind let's hear it.

> *Ben hesitates.*

Go on, let's get it out there. Let's talk about it.

> *Ben takes a deep sigh.*

BEN. Okay, well—

ALICE. *(Immediately cuts him off.)* Forget it.

> *Alice exits upstage center.*
>
> *She returns, dialing a phone.*

BEN. What are you doing?

ALICE. I thought we were going to try and rise to the occasion but I guess not. They're going to be disappointed.

BEN. *(Alarmed.)* You're calling them?

ALICE. I'm not going to subject them to a man not willing to look his best.

BEN. What are you going to say, Alice? *(Then.)* What *the heck* are you going to say?

ALICE. I'm going to say they shouldn't come. *(Finally hangs up the phone.)* No answer.

BEN. They're on their way.

> *Alice stifles a sob as she exits stage right.*

(Calls after her.) There wasn't anything you could've said.

 Ben looks for some way to be helpful.

 He turns off the television.

(Calls out.) I turned the TV off.

 Ben contemplates the tray a moment.

(Musing.) "Got yer carrots, got yer celery sticks."

 Calling out to Alice again—

Thinking we should put out some crackers?

 Alice suddenly bursts into the room, furious.

ALICE. Did you go to King Kullen today?

BEN. What?

ALICE. *(Teeth clenched.)* Did you? Go to? King Kullen?

 Ben realizes he may be in trouble here.

BEN. *(Attempt at "so what?" defiance.)* I got some frozen pizzas.

ALICE. You got some frozen pizzas at King Kullen? And did you get the toilet scrubby?

BEN. The—?

ALICE. The thing—the brush—for the bathroom.

BEN. No.

ALICE. Do you have some kind of death wish or something?

BEN. I forgot they had those there!

ALICE. What are you talking about? It's a superstore.

BEN. I know!

ALICE. If you can't get a toilet scrubby at a twenty-two-aisle King Kullen superstore, where the hell do you think you're going to get it?

BEN. I don't know!

ALICE. What is wrong with you? I must have told you fourteen times they had scrubbies there. *What the hell is wrong with you?!*

BEN. I got lost, okay? I got lost and I couldn't find anything. I don't know the last time you went to King Kullen on a Sunday but, it has gotten really crowded. Everyone's stacked on top of one another. Like goats. Like animals. And they moved the freezers around somehow and changed the cereal section so I didn't know where I was half the time. I got turned around, I couldn't find the front checkouts, I couldn't see over all the heads. I kept walking around and ending up in a corner by men wrapping meat in brown paper. I'm sorry but I couldn't stay to look for housewares. I had to get out of there! I'll try to get it tomorrow.

ALICE. "Tomorrow"? They're on their way.

BEN. *(Outrage.)* So what?! So *what* they're on their way?! I'm not going to let them push us around this time! We've been doing fine all this time without the Christopher Cross and the penny loafers and we've been doing fine without that thing for the toilet so that is just going to have to do.
(Outrage dissipating.) And if that doesn't do, if that isn't good enough for them well then so be it. We'll just try and remember to keep the lid down.

ALICE. "Keep the—"?

BEN. The top of the seat looks fine. I can double-check but, I'm pretty sure it's clean on top. We'll just keep the lid down.

ALICE. She'll lift it up! She's going to lift it up! *(Then.)* He'll laugh and smile and talk to us about some new movie from Denmark while she sneaks off to the bathroom…

BEN. *(Talking over, "don't say it.")* Alice—

ALICE. …locks the door, lifts the lid…

BEN. Alice, I mean it—

ALICE. …and with big white eyes, kneels down…

BEN. Alice—!

ALICE. …*and drinks.*

BEN. There's no reason to think that that's what she was—

ALICE. What was it then, Ben? What was that noise?

BEN. She said she was bulimic.

ALICE. That's not the sound we heard and you know it.

BEN. We don't know that that—

ALICE. I KNOW WE NEED THAT SCRUBBY.

BEN. *(Angry, determined.)* Okay fine.

> *Ben exits upstage center.*

Alice crosses and stands outside the kitchen door.

ALICE. *(Looking into the kitchen.)* What are you doing?

Ben reappears holding a small wooden dish brush.

What are you doing with that?

Ben starts to cross stage left but Alice blocks his way.

Ben, answer me!

BEN. I'm going to the bathroom!

ALICE. Not with that dish utensil you aren't!

BEN. It's a stupid brush!

ALICE. It's a nineteen-dollar Merlin Brothers dish utensil Ben— and it's not going anywhere near that toilet.

BEN. Okay then.

Ben tries to snap the brush handle in two.

Alice tries to stop him.

ALICE. Ben! Ben stop that! Don't break it! Ben!

There's a scuffle, but soon Ben is able to turn away from her. He struggles intensely trying to break the little brush. But the handle's too small for him to get enough leverage.

BEN. ArrHHHHH!!!!

Ben bellows in rage as the effort drives him to his knees.

(Losing steam.) Guruhhhh…!!! unnnh…!!!

Finally, he gives up and…

ALICE. Okay… Why don't we just…?

…gives Alice the brush. She exits.

*Ben is sagging and needs Cool J to get him to his feet. In a voiceover, he sings a few lines from the hip-hop song from earlier.**

Ben momentarily goes into the bathroom before reemerging.

(Calling out, reassuring "like I said.") The top of the seat looks fine.

No response.

Ben goes to the couch and turns on the TV.

Eventually he half reclines into his "lounge."

Alice reenters, notes Ben, and, with some reluctance, comes to sit on the arm of the couch.

ALICE. What's this?

BEN. Discovery Channel. *The Siege of Leningrad.*

ALICE. Oh, right. *(Then.)* That's…?

BEN. World War Two.

A beat as Alice tries to watch.

ALICE. *(Flat.)* This is like…watching sand grow.

BEN. What?

ALICE. Nothing's happening, Ben.

BEN. Seriously?

ALICE. *(Overlapping.)* Really ever, really.

BEN. *(Overlapping.)* It's the largest military encirclement of all time.

ALICE. *(Overlapping.)* No, that's not—

BEN. *(Overlapping.)* The city's surrounded. They're eating horses to survive.

ALICE. *(Overlapping.)* That's not what I'm saying—

BEN. *(Overlapping.)* Pretty soon they'll start eating each other.

ALICE. *(Cutting through.)* Here! I meant here! The sand is here!

BEN. What—?

ALICE. Nothing's happening! Nothing's happening to us!

BEN. Hey, hey—

ALICE. *(Losing it.)* THE SAND IS HERE! THE SAND IS EVERYWHERE! The ROOM is filling up with SAND! The carpet, Ben! The couch! The windows! We're getting BURIED by the sand!

Ben is confused and spooked by her outburst.

BEN. Wait, WHAT? What are you talking about? There's no sand, Alice! NO SAND! NO SAND!

ALICE. I—I—I just—

BEN. NO SAND!

Her episode is over. Alice sits back down on the couch.

ALICE. I know. I'm sorry. I—

> *Ben is still in crisis mode—*

BEN. *(Insisting.)* NO SAND!

ALICE. Okay, I'm okay. I'm sorry.

BEN. It's alright.

> *Ben starts to catch his breath now—*

(Mocking.) "The room's filling up with sand."

> *Ben chuckles at the absurdity.*

Oh my god, that was so nuts.

ALICE. *(Flat.)* It was an analogy.

BEN. *(Soothing.)* No, I know, sweetheart, I know. It's over. You're fine now.

> *Alice sniffs.*

ALICE. Ben?

BEN. Yes, sweetheart?

ALICE. You won't be mean to me tonight, will you?

> *Ben looks at her.*

BEN. Mean to you? Of course not. When am I mean to you?

ALICE. No, you're not.

BEN. Hold on now, tell me. I want to know when you think I'm being mean.

ALICE. I don't think that. I was just being—you know—I was just worrying.

BEN. Of course. *(Sincere.)* Because—and this might be a corny thing to say but, I don't think I ever *could* be mean to you, you know? I just love you too much.

ALICE. Yeah. *(Then.)* I think what I was talking about is that in certain situations you can get nervous or uncomfortable and sometimes you get frustrated and take it out on me because you know I won't fight back.

> *Ben lets go of her.*

BEN. Wow.

ALICE. Only sometimes.

BEN. *(Defensive.)* No. That's how you feel.

ALICE. You know what I'm talking about though, right?

BEN. Well, I speak English, Alice. I know what "mean" means.

ALICE. Ben—

BEN. I guess all I can say in my defense is that I really, really think you're wrong about that and—

ALICE. Look, I didn't say—

BEN. —and also, please forgive me, but you're not exactly one to talk, are you Alice? So why don't we just leave it at that.

ALICE. What does that mean? You think I'm mean to you?

> *Ben isn't exactly sure what he meant, so he goes on the offensive. He reverts to shouting and "meanness."*

BEN. So wait a second, first, you said I don't do anything but now, you're saying all I do is run around being mean all the time. I'm confused. Which is it?

ALICE. I didn't say all you did was run around—

BEN. No, I'm curious. I want to know: is it I don't *do anything*? Or is it that I'm *mean*?

ALICE. Ben, you're overreacting—

BEN. *(Talking over her.)* I want to understand your logic so tell me: mean or nothing? Am I nothing or am I mean?

ALICE. You alternate!

BEN. *(Stung.)* That's fine. Okay. Now I know.

> *He returns to the TV.*

ALICE. I am not going to apologize!

> *She storms out into the kitchen. Sound of Alice slamming cabinet doors, banging silverware, etc.*
>
> *Alice reappears, crosses downstage, and sits on the arm of the couch.*

I'm sorry.

> *Ben turns off the TV.*

BEN. *(Guilty.)* It's not that… I'm not trying to be mean.

ALICE. I know.

BEN. I'm sorry.

ALICE. I'm sorry, too.

> *Beat.*

> *Suddenly—*

(Happy, laughing.) What's wrong with us?!

BEN. What do you mean?

ALICE. I mean this happens every time they come over. We get anxious and paranoid and then we start fighting and it's just a complete waste of time.

> *Alice's optimism is infectious.*

BEN. I know! It's crazy.

ALICE. This is what people do. Every now and then you have other people over.

BEN. It's true.

ALICE. And of course it's going to be scary not knowing what's going to happen, but you know what? And I really mean this: it's worth it.

BEN. It usually turns out fine anyways.

ALICE. They're dropping by. That's it. We sit around. We talk. We drink some wine.

BEN. We listen to how "great" everything is going.

ALICE. She doesn't always say things are "great."

BEN. No, I know. *(Can't think of anything.)* She's just…she's just…

ALICE. And maybe they are doing great? We're doing pretty good too, you know, right?

BEN. Yeah, no, definitely: it'll be good.

ALICE. I'm going to be really upbeat and friendly.

BEN. And beautiful.

ALICE. Thank you sweetheart. *(Then.)* I'll be beautiful and you'll be handsome and funny and we have jalapeño poppers and fresh-ground Easter Blend if people want it, and if, at some point, things start to get out of hand, you'll immediately deal with it.

BEN. Great.

ALICE. You won't be pushy about it or like a bully at all, you'll just be clear about what can and can't be happening. Okay?

BEN. Good.

ALICE. How's that sound?

BEN. Fine.

ALICE. I think it sounds like a lot of fun.

BEN. Well, we'll see…

ALICE. You'll be very firm with them if need be.

BEN. I'll certainly try to get my points across.

ALICE. I know you will, sweetheart.

>*As the fear begins to creep back in, Ben begins to bristle.*

BEN. I'll *try* Alice. Whether or not they *listen* is another story.

ALICE. Well, then you'll make them listen if you have to.

BEN. I'll certainly object strenuously, Alice, but I don't know how I'm actually going to make someone listen.

ALICE. You just said you'll "put your foot down"?

BEN. Of course I'll put my foot down! Of course I'll put my foot down! But that's not the only issue. That's not all we're up against.

ALICE. What do you mean?

BEN. I mean he's stronger than me, okay? In case you've forgotten, he's just a little bit stronger!

ALICE. That's not true. You just weren't prepared. You looked into the bedroom, you saw that he was, you know—

BEN. With you.

ALICE. Right. He and I—

BEN. In the bedroom.

ALICE. Whatever you want to call it. You looked in and you saw and you panicked.

BEN. NO! I didn't panic. I didn't—but—but—you can't just do whatever you want!

ALICE. Okay so, this time—if it even happens again, which I doubt—instead of just watching from the doorway and screaming, you'll get mad and come in after him. You'll murder him with your fists.

BEN. No, no, no.

ALICE. You can do it, Ben.

> *Ben begins to completely lose it. His childish terror and his impotent indignation rise together.*

BEN. NO! I CAN'T! There's too much to keep track of. Trying to keep him contained? Worrying about my shoes while she sneaks off to the toilet?

ALICE. Ben—

BEN. Thinking of things to talk about?

ALICE. Sweetheart—

BEN. Running around like a-a-a cocker spaniel or something, trying to keep things under control, while they just sit there, thinking I'm some kind of curly Greek, ridiculous Greek LOSER?

ALICE. Ben—

BEN. I mean, who are these people?! Where did they come from?! What the heck do they want from us?!

ALICE. They're our best friends.

BEN. I know but— *(Final spasm of outrage before he exhausts.)* How dare they? How dare they?! HOW DARE THEY?!

ALICE. *(Calming.)* Okay, let's sit down on the couch.

BEN. Sorry, I just get—

ALICE. I know.

BEN. —fed up, you know?

ALICE. I know.

> *Ben collects himself. Alice rubs his back.*

You're only half Greek, Ben.

BEN. *("Stop babying me.")* Alice, *come on.* Look at me with all these… *(Self-loathing, referring to his hair.)* …stupid twisty spirals.

ALICE. Well, it doesn't matter to me really much at all.

BEN. Thanks.

> *Ben's outburst has left him raw, sniffling back tears.*
>
> *Alice observes him coolly. Then—*

ALICE. So, what do we do? Not answer?

BEN. I wish. Hide under the couch…

ALICE. I'm serious.

> *Ben looks at her, considering her proposal.*

BEN. They'd know we're in here, Alice.

ALICE. Not if we're quiet. They wouldn't be sure.

> *Another beat.*

BEN. You'd never forgive me.

ALICE. That's not true.

> *Ben studies her.*

BEN. Be honest.

ALICE. No, it would be a joint decision. *(Then.)* What do you think? *(Then.)* Or we could just, you know, suck it up, take a deep breath, and go through with it?

BEN. *(Appearing to "agonize.")* Yeah, it's a tough one. Both ideas are so great…

ALICE. *(Checks her watch.)* But we have to decide, because.

BEN. Right, okay, to me? I like the just-us kinda coziness, you know? To me? That's the slightest sorta tiebreaker—over the—over them coming over. *(Then.)* But what do you think?

ALICE. I think…

BEN. Be honest.

ALICE. *(Bristling.)* Stop telling me to be—I'm being honest. *(Choosing her words.)* I think that, at least for now, you… *(Correcting herself.)* …and me—not just—it's both of us…aren't ready for company.

BEN. I hate to say it but I think you might be right. Maybe if the music and the scrubby and the shoes fit but yeah. We're not ready.

ALICE. So that's it then? We don't answer?

BEN. I don't think so.

ALICE. Right. We just sit here and…

BEN. I mean: yeah. *(Double checking.)* Unless you?

ALICE. No, this is good. That's fine. *(Wants to mean it.)* I'm relieved.

> *Ben exhales.*

BEN. *(Sincerely means it.)* Totally relieved.

ALICE. Good.

BEN. *(Excitement flooding in.)* And besides, if we're really being honest? It's hard to go wrong with a nice evening in.

ALICE. Yeah.

> *Ben turns on the TV.*

BEN. *(Referring to the TV channel guide.)* What's great is…I think there's going to be some old *Simon & Simons*… Here it is… Yeah: it's a marathon.

ALICE. Later we should call and say we got the dates screwed up.

BEN. Good.

ALICE. And I think we should reschedule.

BEN. Oh definitely, I agree. I don't think we should cancel, I never meant we should cancel.

> *Alice watches.*
>
> *Beat.*
>
> *Alice exits.*
>
> *Beat.*
>
> *Ben looks up suddenly. Like he heard something.*
>
> *He crosses to the downstage right window. As he looks out, those "outside" sounds come in once again. This time they are louder.*
>
> *Alice reappears upstage. She's heard the sounds too.*
>
> *The sounds build and blend and grow louder and louder, until…*
>
> *A sudden silence.*
>
> *Sound of a doorbell.*
>
> *Ben turns and looks back upstage at Alice.*
>
> *She looks back at him. A light of challenge in her eyes, before she calls out—*

ALICE. Coming!

> *Blackout.*

SCENE TWO

Theme music from a show like Marathon Man[*] *plays a few moments before—*

Lights up on the living room a little bit later.

The guests have arrived.

Ben and Alice sit on one couch while Danny and Doris, an ordinary-type couple, sit on the other. They're drinking white wine. Some snacks on the table between them.

The party seems to be going fine.

Ben is in the middle of an amusing anecdote.

BEN. …and I'm not saying anything. What can I say? There's nothing. I'm just—you know—gonna keep my head down and try to get through it. So I make my way over to the next aisle. And I turn and I look around the corner and way down at the other end, I see… *(Trying to remember.)* …the—you know, that counter thing—the booth?—where they try to help you?

DANNY. The "information kiosk."

BEN. Right, the kiosk! So I see the kiosk and it looks like there's a guy in there and I'm thinking, "Finally. FINALLY." You know? And it's at the end of "Plastics, Wraps, and Foil" so there's a nice flow; no clumping, no children. It's pretty clear. So, I start moving down the right-hand side of the aisle toward the kiosk.

DANNY. I don't like where this is going.

BEN. *(Laughing.)* So, I start down the aisle and I'm about halfway down when these two ladies stop their carts and start talking to each other. Just suddenly stop and start talking—for no reason— I guess they knew each other. Anyway, the problem is they were coming from opposite directions and they've angled their carts out, so the entire right-hand side of the aisle is cut off, and the left-hand side is almost completely cut off too. And this is all

---

25

happening like—seven feet in front of me. So now I'm thinking to myself, "This is not good." I'm gonna have to backtrack and try my chances through the "Soups and Condiments." So, I start to turn around, when I realize, right behind me, is a guy in one of those huge wheelchairs. The big, wide black ones with the side-saddle bags, the engine, and the eating tray? This guy must've been right behind me the whole time! And he's coming right at me. So, now I'm thinking: crap. What the heck do I do? So—

ALICE. *(To Doris.)* Doris? Is that cushion bothering you? *(To Ben.)* I'm sorry to interrupt.

DORIS. No, it's fine.

ALICE. Because you can just move it if you want.

DORIS. It's fluffy. I love it.

ALICE. Good. *(To Ben.)* I'm sorry, honey. *(Prompting.)* So, the old ladies stopped and…

BEN. They weren't "old ladies," Alice.

ALICE. I thought you said they were elderly?

BEN. What are you talking about—? They were in their forties.

ALICE. *("Continue.")* Anyway, the ladies scared you and the wheelchair came from behind…

BEN. They didn't scare me. They blocked the aisle.

ALICE. Okay.

BEN. They all of a sudden stopped and jammed their carts together and basically created a wall.

ALICE. Okay.

BEN. It wasn't about my being scared of them, it was about not being able to get around.

ALICE. Okay. I'm sorry.

DORIS. Sounds terrible. Being all boxed in like that.

> *Alice touches Ben's hand sympathetically.*

ALICE. Sweetheart.

BEN. *("To be clear.")* It was more like, "What the heck's going on?" you know?

DORIS. Of course. It sounds disorienting.

Ben can't remember where he left off.

BEN. Anyway, so wait…uh…

DANNY. *(Gently putting an end to things.)* You made it. That's what matters. You escaped the haunted supermarket.

Laughter.

Then…

I really like this wine, though.

ALICE. Oh good.

DANNY. *(To Doris.)* Did you try this?

DORIS. I did try it, yes.

ALICE. It's an Italian Pinot Grigio.

DANNY. *(Sniffing the wine.)* Um-hm. Few different notes here… *(Sniffs again.)* Pear. Honeydew.

ALICE. It's Italian.

DANNY. *(More sniffing.)* Wet gravel.

ALICE. It's Italian. *(Looking around.)* Wait, where's the bottle? *(Trying to remember the name.)* Casa di Treppo or—Casa di— *(Then.)* Something Italian. I read somewhere that more people are starting to drink European white wines. So I thought it might be nice.

DANNY. I like it.

ALICE. I think it's Casa di Trippo, or—

Alice stands.

Let me check.

DORIS. Oh Alice, please don't bother.

Alice hovers, uncertain.

ALICE. It's not a bother. It's just in the kitchen.

DORIS. *(Shrugs.)* Okay.

Alice is embarrassed by her over-enthusiasm.

ALICE. *(Making fun of her "crazy" self.)* Do-I-sit-or-do-I-stand-do-I-sit-or-do-I-stand?

DORIS. Why don't you sit?

Alice obeys and sits.

ALICE. Right, who cares what it's called? I'm just glad you like it.

> *Beat.*

DANNY. So. Here we are.

> *Beat.*

ALICE. Yeah!

DANNY. Finally.

> *Ben stands and makes a toast.*

BEN. *(Awkward.)* I just want to say: welcome and we love you and let's see…yeah *finally* is right.

> *Laughter.*

Anyway, welcome. That's it. Thanks.

DORIS. Thank you for having us.

ALICE. That was sweet.

> *Danny sets down his wine glass and stands.*

DANNY. *(Gestures to Ben.)* C'mere.

> *Danny goes to Ben and hugs him.*

Thanks.

> *Both Alice and Doris "awww" in appreciation. Danny sits down, wiping his eye.*

DORIS. That was nice, Ben. You made Danny cry.

DANNY. Well, we've missed you guys.

ALICE. We've missed you too.

DANNY. It seems like forever since the last time we were here.

ALICE. I know.

> *Beat.*

DORIS. What happened?

> *Beat.*

ALICE. What do you mean?

DORIS. Why is it so hard to get together?

ALICE. I know! Ugh. Are we too busy? Is that it?

BEN. *(The expert.)* Yeah, it's such an interesting question. I think what happens is that we get to a place where our schedules can become so—

DANNY. *(Mutters skeptically.)* I don't know… *(To Ben, referring to his interruption.)* Oh sorry, buddy.

BEN. That's okay. *(Then.)* No, I was just saying, and it's funny, I've actually given this a fair amount of thought—

DANNY. It's fear. *(Then.)* Don't you think? Fear of what you don't know. Fear of what you can't control—which, if we're being honest is pretty much everything.

ALICE. That is so weird. We were just talking about this like twenty minutes ago.

BEN. *(Low warning.)* Alice.

ALICE. What? We were.

BEN. *(Covering.)* I think it was a lot longer than twenty minutes.

ALICE. *(To Danny.)* We totally agree with you.

DANNY. We get set in our ways. We get into a groove. With our lives. That's fine, it happens. But you don't want to live in the groove, do you? Otherwise, after a while, you can't see over the sides.

    Alice nods in sincere agreement. Then—

ALICE. That is so true. Why do we do that?

DANNY. Well—

BEN. *(The expert again.)* There are so many reasons, Alice. I mean, it's… *(Restarting.)* Fear, oh man, fear is such a big one… *(Restarting again.)* And—and now with everything that's going on these days with all the crime and the drugs and Fallujah.

DANNY. Right.

BEN. I read somewhere that they think someone may be trying to kill off all the honeybees. Eliminate them entirely, once and for all.

DANNY. To what end?

BEN. Exactly.

DANNY. But why would someone want to kill all the bees?

BEN. No one knows. That's one of things that's so chilling about it. The senselessness.

DANNY. Right.

    Alice attempts to bring the conversation to a conclusion.

ALICE. But yes: everyone is afraid.

> *Beat.*

(Referring to the music.) This is one of the few songs I ever learned for the guitar.

> *She sings a few lines of a song like Cat Steven's "Moonshadow."*

BEN. Doesn't she have a nice voice?

DANNY. Um-hm.

BEN. I always tell her she should try out for one of those open-mike-night thingys.

ALICE. *("Don't embarrass me.")* Ben, please.

BEN. No, you should try.

> *They all listen to Alice sing a bit more of the song. At one point, Danny joins her.*
>
> *Then—*

DORIS. Isn't he Muslim?

ALICE. Who?

DORIS. Him? The—?

ALICE. Cat Stevens?

DORIS. He's a Muslim now?

> *Alice shoots a look at Ben. Cat Stevens was his idea.*

ALICE. I…don't think so.

DANNY. He is. He converted.

BEN. Not that that means anything?

DORIS. Oh no, no, no—

BEN. Because in America—

DORIS. Of course, of course. Everyone should feel free to worship their own particular…

DANNY. Deity.

DORIS. Of course. *(Then.)* No, I was just remembering it.

> *Beat.*

ALICE. I was going to put on some Christopher Cross but I don't know where it went.

DORIS. This is fine.

  Beat.

DANNY. We saw Chris Cross play out at Jones Beach a few summers back. Incredible evening. Saw every star in the sky. Almost didn't have to wear a jacket.

ALICE. Wow.

DANNY. The arrangements. The pacing. At the encore when he sang "Sailing"? And the strings came in? *(Trailing off.)* Those violins…

ALICE. Wow.

BEN. *(Low, to Alice.)* Did you check the little case by the stereo?

ALICE. *(Terse.)* Did I look in the CD case for the missing CD? Yes, I did.

  Beat.

DORIS. *("Moving on.")* I love your shoes by the way.

BEN. Oh—thanks.

ALICE. *(Making light.)* There was a lot of discussion about the shoes.

BEN. We went back and forth about wearing loafers but they didn't fit great and so.

DORIS. Well they look very comfy with the stripes.

BEN. I mean, if you have to choose between how you look and how you feel?

DORIS. *(Nodding, agreeable.)* You choose comfort. A lot of people do these days.

BEN. I choose not having heel blisters for no reason other than, "Hey, everybody, look at my loafers."

DORIS. Got it. Good for you. *(Then.)* I'm sorry what were we talking about?

DANNY. Christopher Cross—

ALICE. *(Overlapping.)* Did you guys see that new show the other night?

DANNY. Which one?

ALICE. That new one? With that guy who's so famous?

DANNY. Val Kilmer?

ALICE. No, not Val Kilmer. He used to be on another show and he wasn't the star but he was the funny costar? He was very funny? Played a policeman?

BEN. *(Helping out.)* Oh, yeah.

DANNY. *(Not ringing any bells.)* Hm.

ALICE. Anyway, he has a new show and this time he's the star of it and he plays a veterinarian.

DANNY. Huh.

ALICE. Did you see it?

DORIS. No.

DANNY. Was it good?

ALICE. I haven't seen it either. That's why I was wondering.

DANNY. Oh, right. *(Then.)* Yeah, I don't know.

BEN. Is it a comedy?

ALICE. I think so. Each week he meets different people who come into the clinic with their pets.

BEN. *(Already amused.)* Haha. I like it.

ALICE. *(Off Ben's approval.)* Maybe we can watch this week's?

BEN. When is it?

ALICE. Sunday, 8:30.

BEN. That's *The Bernie Mac Show.*

ALICE. Well, we can record and watch it after?

BEN. Let's talk about it later.

> *Alice turns back to Danny and Doris.*

ALICE. Anyway. *(Back to Ben.)* What is there to talk about later? We set the recorder to "record" and record it.

BEN. It's not the same. Alice just…

ALICE. Anyway.

> *Beat.*

DORIS. *(Laughing.)* You guys are hysterical.

ALICE. What do you mean?

DORIS. I mean you're hysterical. You both seem so happy.

ALICE. Thank you. *(To Ben.)* You hear that, sweetheart?

BEN. Yeah, I guess we're pretty good. *(Referring to Alice, joking.)* I mean, it's not the easiest thing in the world but…

> *Laughter.*

DANNY. Looks pretty easy from where I'm sitting.

> *Laughter.*

DORIS. *(To Danny.)* Ugh, you're such a pig.

ALICE. *(Playing along.)* Why, Danny: I never knew you cared.

> *Danny smiles.*

DANNY. Come on, Alice. You knew.

DORIS. *(To Ben, scolding.)* Are you going to let them get away with that?

> *Ben puts his hand on Doris's lap.*

BEN. I don't know what you're talking about, baby.

> *Laughter.*
>
> *Fades, then—*

DORIS. *(Shudders at the thought.)* Ecch.

BEN. *(Quickly.)* I know.

DORIS. *(Moving past it.)* But you guys are doing okay?

BEN. Oh, yeah. Definitely.

ALICE. Yes.

DORIS. Good.

BEN. *(Repeating his joke.)* I mean, it's not the easiest thing in the world but…

> *Less laughter than before.*

DORIS. But you're doing good and that's good.

ALICE. Yes.

DORIS. Good.

> *Alice and Ben give each other a sidelong look. They know what Doris is asking for here.*

BEN. *(Overlapping.)* How—?

ALICE. *(Overlapping.)* How have you guys been doing?

DORIS. Well, I'd have to say pretty great.

ALICE. *(Faking excitement.)* Oh my god: that's great!

DORIS. It's been kind of an amazing time for us.

ALICE. That's amazing.

DORIS. It's been really amazing.

ALICE. *(Trying to end it.)* That is so great.

DORIS. Thanks, Alice.

> *Doris waits to be asked. But if they won't ask…*

Danny got Swiss Madrid.

ALICE. Oh my god, that's amazing! *(Then.)* "Swiss Madrid"? Is that a big one?

BEN. *(Quiet.)* Huge.

DORIS. Huge.

DANNY. Pretty big, yeah.

BEN. Huge.

DORIS. Huge account.

BEN. Huge.

DORIS. Comes with a Cozumel time-share.

ALICE. Wow, oh my god. Congratulations.

> *Catatonic with jealousy, Ben stands with a frozen grin.*

BEN. Well, I guess it's my turn now. *(Imitating Danny from earlier.)* C'mere you.

> *Danny doesn't rise, however. He offers a high five.*

Congratulations.

> *Ben high-fives and makes a move to Doris but backs off quickly when she sips her wine and looks away.*
>
> *Sitting down, Ben knocks the TV remote off the table.*

ALICE. Watch it, Ben.

BEN. What?

> *Alice puts the remote back.*

ALICE. You knocked this over.

BEN. Sorry.

ALICE. Be careful.

BEN. Sorry. *(Then.)* But yeah. Swiss Madrid.

DANNY. Thank you.

> *The conversation lulls into a prolonged silence. Then—*

DORIS. Such a sweet neighborhood.

ALICE. Oh, thank you. Yeah.

DORIS. Very tidy. Safe and quiet.

ALICE. Um-hm. It is quiet.

BEN. *(Rueful.)* Most of the time.

ALICE. Oh, it's not that bad. *(Explaining to Danny and Doris.)* There are some boys that play whiffle ball, but it's been quiet lately. *(To Ben.)* You know I haven't seen them in a while. Maybe it's spring break or something?

BEN. What are you talking about? They were there two days ago. *(To Danny and Doris.)* They're always screaming and running around out there.

DANNY. Where? In the yard?

BEN. You believe it?

DANNY. You let them on your property?

> *Sensing Danny's disapproval, Ben backtracks—*

BEN. No, no. Not on the property.

ALICE. That's not true. *(To Danny.)* They use our driveway as an outfielding area.

> *Ben turns on Alice.*

BEN. It's "outfield-er," Alice, not "outfield-ing."

ALICE. Sorry.

BEN. *(Rolling his eyes.)* "Outfielding."

ALICE. *(Bristles.)* I don't know what it's called.

BEN. *(Mocking.)* "What position did you play in high school?" "Who, me? I was an 'outfielding.'"

ALICE. *(Angry.)* I said I didn't know, Ben.

BEN. *(Catching himself.)* Sorry.

ALICE. Um-hm.

DORIS. What do they say?

BEN. Who?

DORIS. The kids on your lawn? What do they say?

BEN. I don't know. Those stupid baseball chants, I guess. I try not to listen.

DORIS. No, what do they say to you? What happens when you tell them to stop?

Ben doesn't have a good answer.

BEN. Oh I see. You know, it's funny, I've been so busy I haven't had the time to uh.

DORIS. Ben.

BEN. I know.

DORIS. They're just going to keep doing it.

BEN. I know, I know.

DANNY. If I were you I'd say something.

DORIS. Well we know you'd say something, Danny.

DANNY. I would.

DORIS. At the very least, he'd say something.

Laughter.

DANNY. I went to a lecture in the city last week. Yali Kruyff was speaking at a bookstore. You know Yali? Wrote *Nothing Worth Knowing* and *How to Make Love in Lisbon*?

ALICE. Oh yeah. He's great.

DANNY. She talked a lot about the power of just doing. Overcoming doubts, taking action. That kind of thing.

ALICE. Huh.

BEN. *(Overlapping.)* Huh.

DANNY. I remember she said—she said a lot of things but at some point I had drifted back to nonfiction to meet a friend but was still half-listening to the lecture through the shelves when she said and I'll never forget it— *(Quotes.)* "In a town made of knives, the butchers run for mayor."

A beat for Ben and Alice to digest.

ALICE. Huh.

BEN. *(Overlapping.)* Huh.

DANNY. I wish you guys had been there.

ALICE. *(Looks at Ben.)* Sounds like it could've been helpful.

BEN. Don't look at me. You said you were going to find the parents' number over there.

ALICE. I did. I put it on the refrigerator.

BEN. The—?

ALICE. Go see for yourself.

BEN. *(Bristling.)* Okay—well—you can't just put it on the refrigerator and think I'm magically going to know about it!

ALICE. *(Rolling her eyes.)* Oh, for Christ's sake…

>   *Doris laughs again.*

DORIS. I love this.

ALICE. Sorry, sorry. We've been sort of grumpy with each other lately. *(To Ben.)* Haven't we?

BEN. I'm sorry. It's my fault.

ALICE. *(Overlapping.)* No, it's been both of us.

BEN. No, no, I've been, I don't know what…

ALICE. *(Prompting.)* Disappointing.

>   *Ben nods, agreeable.*

But I've been. It's not like I haven't been…?

BEN. *(Overlapping.)* Really bad.

ALICE. *(Overlapping.)* Myself so. *(Explains to Danny and Doris.)* Normal couple stuff. Trust, intimacy, blah blah. *(Making light.)* "How to ask for what you want in a way that's generous to yourself but respectful to your partner?" Blah blahbity blah.

BEN. Haha. Right. Borrring! *(To be clear.)* But you don't mean "intimacy" like "sex" or "sexual" or as in "sex"? That's not what you—?

ALICE. No. No, no, no. No, not…

BEN. Good. *(Mocks wiping sweat.)* Phew! Haha.

>   *Small beat.*

ALICE. …although sometimes it all sorta runs together, doesn't it?

BEN. *(The expert.)* It does, it does. "I'm a man." Okay great, but what does that mean? "You're a woman," sure, but what does that mean?

"Do this now, don't do that. But hold on now wait a minute, do do that one, because I changed my mind," and so on and so forth.

ALICE. It's complicated.

BEN. It really is.

ALICE. *(Sweet nudge.)* But I think we're figuring it out?

BEN. *(Smiling.)* Absolutely.

ALICE. The key is to keep talking about it. As long as we keep talk—

DORIS. *(Interrupting.)* I meant this.

> Doris indicates a bowl on the table.

I love this.

ALICE. Oh—I'm sorry! *(Laughing at herself.)* And here we were going on and on about all our— *(Referring to the dip.)* But yes—isn't it delicious? Spicy ranch.

DORIS. No, this little bowl here.

ALICE. Oh, good, right?

DANNY. I love the colors.

ALICE. Thank you. They seemed very Mediterranean somehow.

DORIS. Or Mexican even.

ALICE. Definitely. Incan or Mayan.

DORIS. *(Nods as if in agreement.)* Or Mexican.

DANNY. You always have the nicest little tableware-type stuff.

ALICE. I do? What about Doris?

DANNY. What about her?

> Laughter.

DORIS. *(Tight smile.)* Oh, thank you.

DANNY. *(To Ben and Alice.)* She actually just found these wonderful curtains for the study. *(To Doris.)* Where are those from again? Are they Egyptian?

DORIS. You don't need to humor me, Danny.

DANNY. *(Chuckling.)* Uh-oh.

DORIS. "Uh-oh" is right.

BEN. *(Playing along.)* I think you did it this time.

DANNY. Haha. I think you might be right.

DORIS. *(To Ben.)* Did what?

DANNY. Can't criticize the home furnishings.

DORIS. Did what?

BEN. What?

DORIS. *(Pointed.)* What did he do?

> *Ben is a little freaked out by Doris's challenge.*

BEN. W-what did who do? What did Danny do?

> *A tense beat.*

DORIS. The look on your face.

> *She cracks a smile.*

DANNY. She totally had you there!

> *Everyone laughs.*

BEN. I knew there was something! I knew you were doing something!

ALICE. Doris! That's terrible!

BEN. *(Catching his breath.)* It's okay oh my god hilarious. *(Then.)* Reminded me of that—what's that movie? The German movie about the dentist and the diamonds?

> *Ben poorly impersonates Laurence Olivier in* Marathon Man. "Is it safe?"

DANNY. *Marathon Man.* Laurence Olivier.

BEN. That's right. Sir Laurence Olivier…

> *Danny speaks in a far more convincing Olivier accent.*

DANNY. "Is it safe?"

BEN. *(Laughing.)* Ha. Exactly.

ALICE. Is that the movie you meant?

BEN. *(Nods.)* The guy doesn't know what's going on, so Olivier ties him in a chair and tortures him.

DANNY. "Is it safe?"

ALICE. But is that a German movie?

BEN. It's not German it's about Germans. *(Olivier.)* "Is it safe?"

DANNY. "Is it safe?"

BEN. Remember?

ALICE. *(Overlapping.)* No, I know.

BEN. *(Overlapping.)* The New York Nazis?

ALICE. No, I remember.

DANNY. "Is it safe, Ben?"

> *Ben turns back to him.*

BEN. Hm?

> *Danny rises.*

DANNY. "Is it safe?"

BEN. Uh-oh. Look out.

> *Danny crosses to downstage right "sink," washes his hands.*

DANNY. "Is it safe?"

> *Ben does his best to narrate.*

BEN. Here we go with the full on—

DANNY. "Is it safe?"

BEN. He asks Dustin Hoffman, who has no idea what any of this means.

DANNY. "Is it safe?"

> *Danny dries his hands.*

BEN. But Laurence Olivier doesn't care.

> *He just keeps asking, over and over…*

DANNY. "Is it safe?"

BEN. Right, right. Great accent. *(To Alice.)* Isn't that a great accent?

> *Danny crosses upstage center center, his back to the audience now.*

DANNY. "Is it safe?"

BEN. Olivier's had enough, Olivier's lost his patience. So he goes to his briefcase, reaches in and pulls out…

> *Danny pulls out an instrument. He tests it—"rrruh…rrruh."*

…a dentist drill. And now my guy starts to realize that whatever this is? It isn't good.

DANNY. "Is it safe?"

> *Danny turns and approaches Ben.*

BEN. I'm scared now. I'm Dustin Hoffman and I'm scared. But I can't move. I'm strapped to a chair.

Danny moves in and bends over Ben's shoulder.

DANNY. "Open please."

Ben complies, opening his mouth.

Danny stands there with drill poised.

(Final chance.) "Is it safe?"

ALICE. *(Low, uneasy.)* Danny, come on.

Danny turns the drill on—"rrr-UHHHH."

Ben flails, trying to turn his head, but Danny's "Olivier" is too strong, and he moves in with the imaginary drill.

BEN. It's not safe! It's not safe!

DORIS. Very mature you two.

ALICE. Danny!

BEN. *(Terror.)* IT'S NOT SAFE!

Alice has had enough—

ALICE. I said stop it.

Danny straightens and looks over at her.

DORIS. *(Low.)* That's enough.

Danny moves away.

DANNY. *(Still Olivier.)* "I was so close to the pulp."

BEN. *(Real anger.)* If you get any closer to my pulp I'm going after yours!

Danny grins encouragingly.

DANNY. Good. Look forward to it.

Danny sits.

A break in the action as Ben's heart is still racing, gasping for breath, fighting back a full-on panic attack.

ALICE. Sweetie. Are you okay?

Ben does his best to nod encouragingly. Um-hm.

Why don't you take a minute?

DANNY. You okay, bud?

Ben manages his panic and forces a "no biggie" smile.

BEN. No, no, I'm good, I'm good. *(Finally getting his breath back.)* Oh my gosh. Such a great movie.

DANNY. *(Nods.)* Um-hm. Classic.

> *Doris suddenly purses her lips and makes a strange silent gagging motion.*
>
> *It's over quickly—Ben and Alice aren't even sure what they saw.*

ALICE. Are you alright?

DORIS. *(Dismissive.)* I'm sorry. I just remembered something.

ALICE. Oh, no, I hate that.

DORIS. I know.

> *Doris doesn't explain. So Ben asks—*

BEN. What was it?

DORIS. What?

BEN. What did you remember?

DORIS. Oh, nothing. We went to this horrible wedding last weekend…

DANNY. *(Chuckling.)* Oh no; you HAVE to tell them.

DORIS. No, I don't.

DANNY. Yes, you do. *(Explaining.)* It's very funny.

ALICE. We want to hear!

BEN. Tell us!

DORIS. It's not funny at all. It's incredibly embarrassing.

BEN. *(Joking.)* I love embarrassing. Embarrassing's my specialty.

> *Laughter.*

DORIS. No, I can't.

> *Emboldened, Ben impulsively sticks two miniature carrot sticks up his nose.*

BEN. *(Arms wide.)* Look at me! I'm Mr. Embarrassment! Doh-de-doh with the carrots up my—!

> *Alice quickly cuts him off—*

ALICE. *(Immediately.)* Ben.

BEN. *(Immediately.)* So yeah, what happened?

Ben takes the carrot sticks from his nose and holds them in his hands—unsure what to do with them.

DANNY. Come on, Dor.

DORIS. *(Relenting.)* Alright, alright. *(Then.)* Do you know Petty and Dylan Turner?

ALICE. Of course.

DORIS. Do you?

ALICE. *(Caught in a lie.)* Wait—I think maybe I just have heard of them.

DANNY. *("Go on.")* Anyway…

DORIS. Anyway, Petty's sister got married last weekend and they had the reception dinner at Ivanhoe. Very elegant, very restrained. Three forks and lace linens, you know?

ALICE. Sounds beautiful. *(Quiet, to Ben.)* Why don't I take those?

Alice takes Ben's nose carrots and wraps them in a napkin.

DORIS. So at dinner I somehow got seated—this is on the terrace overlooking the golf course—I somehow got seated next to this… overweight teenage boy. And he was unfortunately very loud and very rude and—and he was fat.

Danny makes a small noise.

What?

DANNY. He was younger.

DORIS. He said he was thirteen.

DANNY. He was younger.

Alice stands to leave.

ALICE. *("Get rid of the carrots.")* Excuse me just need to…

Danny begins to rise.

DANNY. Give you a hand?

Ben extends a hand to stop him.

BEN. She's got it.

Alice goes into the kitchen.

DORIS. *(To Danny.)* How do you know how young he was?

DANNY. After the reception, some of us were hanging out behind the tennis courts. He was the only one that didn't know what a "lariat" was.

BEN. Okay, right. *(Then.)* You mean the rope to tie things up in?

DANNY. That's right.

DORIS. Disgusting.

BEN. …what were you doing behind the tennis courts?

DANNY. *(Dismissive.)* Different story.

> *Alice returns and sits.*

(Prompting Doris.) So, you're sitting at the table…

DORIS. *(Continuing.)* That's right. I'm sitting next to this—to him—but I'm going to try and have a nice time and make the best of it. And at first, it was fine; Billy Munion was there telling this very funny story about a *Viet-namese* man who thought he could drink saltwater. And I can see him out of the corner of my eye pawing through the basket of dinner rolls, but I just try and ignore him. So, we're sitting there about ten minutes when they start serving the soup.

DANNY. A carrot-ginger soup.

DORIS. Heavy cream. Some sort of vegetable stock. Anyway: it was bright orange.

DANNY. That was the carrots.

DORIS. So they serve this carrot soup and they put a big bowl down in front of this boy and, of course, he immediately starts playing with it and splattering it everywhere. Getting it all over the linens and the centerpiece. But I'm still trying to ignore it because it's none of my business.

ALICE. Where were the parents?

DORIS. No one knew. Danny eventually found the mother passed out somewhere.

DANNY. She was in the back of the coatroom.

DORIS. I don't know where the husband was.

DANNY. He wasn't around.

DORIS. The point is: no one else is noticing. It feels like nobody cares. And I'm thinking, "Wait a second: a lot of money has been spent here. We should be able to talk to one another and enjoy ourselves without having to look at this." So finally, I very calmly said to him, "Please try and settle down, you're being distracting."

And that was it. I was very calm, I didn't raise my voice. And he proceeds to act like he didn't even hear me. He just bangs his soup spoon all over the tablecloth and laughs at me.

BEN. He thought it was funny?

DORIS. I'd say he seemed to be enjoying my discomfort, yes.

BEN. *(Indignant.)* What the heck is going on with these kids?! I mean, this isn't *Porky's*! You know?!

DORIS. *(Cocks her head.)* …I don't understand the reference.

DANNY. Just keep going.

DORIS. Anyway: so I asked him again. I leaned in and told him to "cut it out." And I guess I must have put my hand on him to stop banging the spoon. He was rapping it on the forks at that point so I was starting to get pretty steamed and…

> *Danny stifles a laugh.*

("Stop.") Danny. *(Then.)* I can't believe you made me tell this story.

BEN. What happened?

DORIS. I was just trying to hold his hand back from the table in order to get him to stop banging and…I guess I was squeezing his arm as well—I don't really remember squeezing it—but…anyway: I hurt his arm.

BEN. You hurt his—? What happened to his arm?

DORIS. Well, it ended up, broken. *(Then.)* Unfortunately.

> *Alice mutters to herself.*

ALICE. Jesus Christ.

> *But Doris hears it.*

DORIS. I thought I was barely touching him, Alice.

> *Alice rallies, plays "supportive."*

ALICE. N-no, of course—it was an accident.

DORIS. It really was. I think what happened was he was wriggling around in his chair so much it kind of threw us off-balance.

ALICE. Of course. You were trying to be helpful.

DORIS. Still—I feel awful about it.

ALICE. *(Overlapping.)* You shouldn't you really shouldn't—

DORIS. *(Overlapping.)* Thank god it was a clean break.

ALICE. *(Overlapping.)* That's good thank god—

DORIS. *(Overlapping.)* Still—it's not really the point, is it?

ALICE. No. I'm sure it must have hurt.

DORIS. *(To Danny.)* Why did you let me tell them that story? Now they think I'm crazy.

ALICE. No, no. We've all done stuff like that.

BEN. Please. Or wanted to do stuff like that.

DORIS. *(Laughs.)* That's terrible, Ben.

BEN. *(Joining her.)* Right? I mean: come on.

DORIS. Well…I admit—and this is horrible—Ben, you're horrible—but I will admit when I heard the sound of his, you know, his arm?

BEN. Uh-huh.

DORIS. Like the snap of an old chair leg?

BEN. Right.

DORIS. I mean…he was such a disgusting little boy.

> *Alice stands.*

ALICE. He-definitely-sounds-it-now-who-likes-jalapeño-poppers?

DANNY. *("I do.")* Ding ding!

> *She stands to leave.*

ALICE. I'll go check the oven.

> *Danny begins to rise.*

DANNY. Give you a hand?

> *Like before, Ben stops him.*

BEN. She's got it.

> *Alice exits.*

> *Ben struggles to come up with something to say…*

I mean, like…I'm trying to remember the last time I even *had* soup.

DANNY. Hm. *(Then.)* Did you cut your hair, Ben?

BEN. Did I?

DANNY. Did anyone?

BEN. No. Why?

DANNY. *(Smiles.)* I was just curious.

Ben fidgets. Senses he's being teased here.

BEN. Right. *(Only half joking.)* I'm Greek and I have curly hair. Sue me.

DANNY. *(Moderately amused.)* Haha. Okay. Calling Judge Judy.

BEN. At least I have hair, so—jealous much?

DANNY. *(Less amused now.)* Haha.

BEN. And at least I don't look like a wrinkly pink ping-pong ball…

DANNY. *(Even less amused.)* Ha. Yeah. Got me there.

Ben worries he's gone too far here. Immediately takes it back.

BEN. But no, I actually really like your. Nice shape, not shiny. Not too much like an egg.

DANNY. Thanks.

Ben crosses his legs revealing his sneakers.

BEN. I'm actually jealous of you.

DANNY. A. D. I. D. A. S. *(Then.)* All day I dream about sex.

Danny turns to Doris.

Adidas.

Doris stares at Ben.

DORIS. Disgusting.

Ben uncrosses his legs, explaining sheepishly—

BEN. …the loafers didn't fit.

DORIS. There's no excuse for it.

BEN. The excuse is my heels being scraped open like a-a hamburger sandwich—

DORIS. I meant me, Ben. What I did.

BEN. Ohhhh, you were talking about the? Breaking the noisy boy's arm thing?

DORIS. That's right.

BEN. *(Magnanimous.)* You know, to me it sounds like it was just one of those things.

DORIS. No. It wasn't.

BEN. Sure it was. I mean, whatever happened to the kids table? They should have had a whole separate table for the—

DORIS. *(Sharp.)* Stop it. *(Then.)* I'm a monster, Ben. Be honest.

BEN. *(Mumbles, flustered.)* …I don't know what you are.

DANNY. Good answer.

> *Doris stands.*

DORIS. May I use your…?

BEN. Of course. It's… *(Then.)* …you know where it is.

> *Doris exits to the bathroom.*

> *Ben watches her go and then turns back, heart racing.*

Holy camoley.

DANNY. *(Agrees.)* Um-hm.

BEN. Ho-leee ca-mooo-leee.

> *A strange "drinking" sound from the offstage bathroom.*

> *Alice appears upstage center. She's hearing it too. She and Ben exchange a concerned glance.*

> *After a moment, the sound stops.*

ALICE. *(Distracted.)* Food soon.

DANNY. Great. Thanks, Al.

> *Alice exits.*

It's going very well by the way.

> *Ben looks at him.*

The party. It's going well.

BEN. You think?

DANNY. *(Nods.)* The food, the wine, the conversations? Her sweater's driving me crazy and you've been hilarious all night.

BEN. Have I?

DANNY. Oh my god. The supermarket story? *Marathon Man* and the carrots up your nose?

BEN. Yeah.

DANNY. That "it's not the easiest thing in the world" thing? We were crying.

BEN. Yeah, that was a good one.

DANNY. "This isn't *Porky's*"? I don't even really *get it* but so funny.

BEN. Okay, good, good.

DANNY. Keep it going, buddy.

BEN. Okay, good. Yeah, yeah, I will, I will.

> *Small beat.*

What was the sweater one?

DANNY. What do you mean?

BEN. You said something about a "sweater"?

DANNY. Did I?

BEN. Some sweater driving you crazy?

DANNY. That's right.

BEN. You meant…?

DANNY. Alice's.

BEN. …oh.

DANNY. With the just one single button thing? Love.

BEN. Yeah.

DANNY. Feels like they're everywhere now.

BEN. I guess they have gotten pretty popular.

DANNY. Down the street, in the elevator, when I'm just trying to eat a sandwich in a restaurant.

BEN. *(Musing, hoping to change the subject.)* Right, right. It's interesting how things catch on. Fashion or sports or even just a funny phrase like… I can't think, but—things you never noticed or even considered are suddenly, like you said—?

DANNY. *(Nods, then.)* Ubiquitous.

BEN. Yes.

DANNY. Pervasive.

BEN. Exactly.

> *Beat.*
>
> *Danny continues in a careful, somewhat vulnerable way.*

DANNY. Hey, Ben? Can I tell you something personal?

BEN. Okay.

DANNY. Something that's been on my mind? Only because you guys were talking about your stuff before? Your own intimacy stuff in such a great way?

BEN. Oh. Sure, of course. Go ahead.

 Danny takes a steadying breath before diving in—

DANNY. It's about the sweaters.

BEN. *(Sighs.)* Okay.

DANNY. I see them, I see them on, and I just have to—not have to, but—I want to—*I lie on them.*

BEN. Lie on them?

DANNY. The sweater. Lower my weight right down on top of it. It moves at first, wriggles around, but eventually it gives up and goes still. *(Then.)* But yeah. That's pretty much it. *(Then.)* I feel…or I feel like I should feel—actually let me not say. *(Then.)* What do you think?

BEN. *(Rolling up his sleeves.)* Okay, so, right. *(Considering.)* Oh my gosh I'm thinking so many things right now…

DANNY. Hm. *(Then.)* Is it creepy?

 Ben doesn't answer.

Is it weird?

 Ben doesn't answer.

Is it funny?

BEN. *(An edge of anger.)* No. It's not funny.

 Danny clocks him.

DANNY. Alright, so what do you think?

 Ben searches for the courage to say…

Come on buddy, hit me. *(Then.)* Hit me.

 Alice returns holding another platter.

ALICE. Okay, it's popper time!

DANNY. Alright, we're ready.

ALICE. *(Noticing.)* She's still in the…?

BEN. Bathroom. Yeah.

DANNY. She'll be out in a sec.

ALICE. Okay. *("Make space for the tray?")* Could you guys…?

Alice sets the tray down and sits.

DANNY. *(Big smile.)* Hey, you guys!

ALICE. Hi, Danny.

DANNY. *(Softly, to Alice.)* Hey, you.

ALICE. *(Presenting.)* So these are my first-time-ever-so-please-forgive-me attempt at jalapeño poppers…

> *Danny takes a jalapeño popper and puts it in his mouth. Again, the "drinking" sound from the offstage bathroom.*
>
> *The sound stops.*

DANNY. *(Referring to the popper.)* Delicious.

ALICE. Oh good. I wasn't sure if they—

> *Danny has another popper as the drinking sound starts again. Finally it ends.*

(Referring to Doris.) …is she alright, you think?

DANNY. Hm?

ALICE. Doris? Is she okay?

DANNY. She's fine. *(Calling.)* Dor?

ALICE. No, no, that's okay.

> *Sound of a toilet flushing.*

DANNY. *(Calling again.)* Dorry?

> *Doris reenters.*

DORIS. I was in the bathroom, Dan.

DANNY. Alice was worried you'd fallen in.

ALICE. *(Quickly.)* That's not true.

> *Doris sits next to Ben on the couch.*

We were just wondering if you're okay?

DORIS. You're so sweet. *(Noticing.)* Oh I see some little snacks here!

ALICE. We went to Applebee's and we loved them so I thought I'd try to make them myself. *(Then.)* Have you ever been to Applebee's? Near the Sports Authority?

DORIS. No.

ALICE. We hadn't either. Ben had his orthodontist so we were in a hurry.

DORIS. I get it. You were desperate. Panicking. All out of options.

ALICE. Yeah.

DORIS. Like a deer caught in traffic.

ALICE. Sort of. *(Dipping a toe in.)* It wasn't bad though. That's the thing. We sorta liked it.

DORIS. I'm sorry. Tell me again what we're talking about?

ALICE. Applebee's. This is what I'm saying. If you just keep an open mind and set aside your prejudices? Applebee's is actually really good.

DORIS. Oh, Alice, please! Come on.

ALICE. N-no, I'm serious.

> *Doris clocks Alice's minor act of defiance with a cool appraising look.*

DORIS. *(Firmness.)* Alice.

> *Alice reluctantly meets her gaze.*

Do you really believe that?

ALICE. *(Laughs, immediately backing down.)* No, not really. I was just kidding.

DORIS. *(Laughing too.)* I thought so. Very funny.

> *Silence.*

> *Ben suddenly leaps to his feet.*

BEN. *(Announces.)* I have an idea!

> *Everyone looks up at him.*

ALICE. What?

BEN. Um.

> *Ben hangs there. He hadn't meant to say this out loud.*

ALICE. What's your idea?

BEN. *(To Danny and Doris.)* One sec.

> *Ben sits down on the couch, trying to speak as privately as possible with Alice.*

I was thinking it might help after all? If I go and get the?

ALICE. *(Not following.)* The what?

BEN. My?

ALICE. *(Losing patience.)* What are you talking about?

BEN. Be right back.

> *Ben stands and quickly exits upstage right into the bedroom.*

ALICE. *(To Danny and Doris.)* No idea.

> *Alice shakes her head.*

(Half to herself.) None.

> *Doris eats a popper.*

DANNY. What do you think, Dor? Delish?

DORIS. I think— *(Still chewing.)* Let me just— *(Now finished.)* I think, Alice you were absolutely right. About being prejudiced and keeping an open mind to new things.

> *Beat as Alice reads her.*

ALICE. So you don't like them?

DORIS. Who?

ALICE. The poppers.

DORIS. No.

> *Doris stands.*

Do you mind if I go get rid of all the greasy goo?

ALICE. T-there's napkins.

DORIS. *(Whisper, as if discussing a "lady problem.")* I wanna wash my hands.

> *Doris exits stage left.*

> *Alice shakes her head.*

DANNY. *(Sincerely encouraging.)* You can't please everyone.

> *He eats another popper.*

ALICE. Ha. I guess not.

> *Alice now realizes she's been left sitting alone with Danny.*

Where did Ben go?

DANNY. I dunno, he just…

> *Danny stands to look but soon sits…now closer to Alice.*

ALICE. *(Calling.)* Ben?

> *Ben doesn't respond.*

Ben?!

Ben doesn't respond.

Weird he's not answering, right?

DANNY. Hm. Maybe he just can't hear you?

ALICE. *(Making light.)* Story of my marriage haha. *(Quickly takes it back.)* No, it's not.

We hear that offstage drinking sound.

This time Alice tries to ignore and talk over it—

Congratulations again on your account.

DANNY. Thank you.

ALICE. Will you still go into the same office or?

DANNY. Same building but on a different floor.

ALICE. Okay. So the exact same commute?

DANNY. That's right.

ALICE. That's great. Makes it easier.

The drinking sound stops.

DANNY. I love that sweater.

ALICE. Cozumel's going to be amazing. *(Then.)* It's Old Navy.

DANNY. *(Overlapping.)* I know.

ALICE. *(Overlapping.)* Ben always talks about the Adirondacks.

DANNY. *(Shrugs.)* Okay, sure.

ALICE. Off into the woods where no one can find us.

DANNY. Right.

ALICE. But obviously there's no comparison.

DANNY. It's all about what you're looking for. Weigh your options, make up your mind and go for it.

ALICE. That's what you do.

DANNY. Sorry?

ALICE. I said that's what you do, right? You just go for it?

DANNY. Life is short, Alice. You can wait around for inspiration or whatever, an epiphany, but life is really short.

ALICE. Not always.

DANNY. It is.

ALICE. Not necessarily.

DANNY. Yes.

ALICE. No, I had an aunt that lived to ninety-seven.

DANNY. *(Gently admonishing.)* Alice.

ALICE. *(Flustered, defending.)* Look. He's—Ben is…
(Starts over.) I remember, he and I, years ago, before the towers, before we knew you guys and we'd just started seeing each other and somehow or other I don't remember who started it but we got really into club dancing. Dancing in clubs. Believe that? Two of us out in the middle of the crowded floor screaming and dancing to whatever, didn't matter: Madonna, Nirvana, LL Cool J. He loved it. We both did.

DANNY. *(Supportive audience.)* I bet. Sounds fun.

ALICE. *(Deflating a little.)* Of course all those places are closed now. Spinners? The Humphrey House? That place off Route 135? They're all gone.

DANNY. There are other dance clubs.

> *Alice bristles at his forwardness.*

ALICE. It's not the same, Danny.

DANNY. *(Backing off.)* No, of course, I don't mean to be. I apologize. *(Sympathizing.)* Time passes, people change, it's painful. *(Half smile.)* Someone should write a song about it.

> *Alice smiles at Danny's wise and gentle teasing.*

ALICE. Hm. Good idea.

DANNY. I think I already have a title. You ready?

ALICE. Sure.

DANNY. Your new song will be called, "That's Over, Now What?"

> *Suddenly, we hear Ben approaching—*

BEN. *(Offstage.)* Alice?

> *Alice stands guiltily as he appears in the upstage right door.*

ALICE. *(Guilty.)* There you are! I was calling you.

> *Offstage toilet flush.*

> *Ben stands there—he senses he interrupted something.*

BEN. I was in the bedroom.

>*Doris returns from the bathroom.*

>*Ben and Alice talk "around" her as she goes back to her place on the couch next to Danny.*

ALICE. Oh, okay.

BEN. Looking for those…

>*Ben surreptitiously indicates his feet.*

…things we were talking about.

ALICE. Oh, great. Good idea!

BEN. But I don't know where.

ALICE. They're not in the closet?

BEN. I didn't see them.

ALICE. Let's go check…

>*Alice exits past Ben—who hasn't moved from the doorway—into the bedroom.*

>*Danny notes Ben looking at him and returns his look.*

DANNY. She was calling for you, buddy.

ALICE. *(Offstage, calling for him.)* Here they are above the humidifier! Come help me reach?

>*Ben goes.*

>*Danny and Doris are left alone.*

>*Doris removes a piece of lint from Danny's pants and says—*

DORIS. Careful.

>*A beat as Danny considers her warning, before responding—*

DANNY. No.

>*Alice reenters from the bedroom and returns to the couch.*

Here she is!

ALICE. Sorry, sorry. *(Vaguely explaining.)* He's just…

DANNY. No problem.

ALICE. *(Offhandedly.)* Everything alright, Doris?

DORIS. Why do you ask?

ALICE. No reason.

DORIS. Then why in the fuck do you keep asking?

> *Alice is stunned like from a slap.*

DANNY. Here he is!

> *Ben reenters, moving stiffly in his new loafers.*

BEN. Sorry, sorry. *(Then.)* I just…

DANNY. No problem.

BEN. *(Referring to his shoes.)* …had to get my freak on.

> *Ben does a painful little dance to showcase his shoes.*

DANNY. *(Ed McMahon.)* Hey-o!

BEN. Let's get the party started!

DANNY. Way ahead of you, buddy.

> *Ben sits.*

BEN. Anyway. Everything alright, Doris?

DORIS. Why?

BEN. No reason.

DORIS. So just another one of your *flaccid* attempts at making conversation?

BEN. *(Backpedaling furiously.)* Wait what? No, I wasn't trying to be—"flaccid," not at all.

DANNY. You know Dor has bulimia, right?

> *Alice snorts skeptically.*

BEN. Ohhh yes. Of course.

> *Ben notes it but is confused and a beat behind.*

Sorry, yeah, I had heard something…

DANNY. What did you hear?

BEN. That…that's what it was?

ALICE. *(Low mutter.)* Jesus Christ.

BEN. So how is it? How's that been going?

DORIS. It's not going well, Ben.

BEN. No?

DANNY. *(Have to agree.)* No.

BEN. I'm sorry.

DORIS. So am I.

> *Alice snaps.*

ALICE. *("Enough.")* Jesus Christ you guys!

> *Everyone turns to her.*

DANNY. What's wrong?

ALICE. I mean Jesus FUCKING Christ!

> *Stunned beat.*

DORIS. *(Explaining.)* She's talking about the music.

ALICE. No, I am not talking about the music! I am talking about THIS. All of this SICK, MANIPULATIVE CUNTING MOTHER FUCKERY!

> *More stunned silence.*
>
> *Until Ben peeps up. Quietly, but oh so proud of her—*

BEN. Totally.

ALICE. *(Overlapping, demanding.)* And what about the music?!

DORIS. *(Simply.)* It went out.

> *Alice listens.*

ALICE. *(Admitting.)* You're right.

DORIS. Which is fine.

DANNY. Sure.

ALICE. Shit.

DORIS. It's alright.

DANNY. It happens.

DORIS. And sometimes nothing is okay.

DANNY. That's right. The silence.

DORIS. Although after a while it usually gets kinda boring.

DANNY. It does. You get restless.

> *Alice shakes her head. These friends of hers are maddening.*

ALICE. What do you guys want?

DANNY. Good question.

DORIS. So you don't have any Christopher Cross?

ALICE. I don't know where it went!

DANNY. She couldn't find it, remember?

DORIS. *(Shrugs.)* That's fine then.

ALICE. Which?

DORIS. You decide.

> *Alice turns to her husband.*

ALICE. Anything, Ben?

> *He's clearly been trying to come up with something to say, some clever or powerful arrangement of words that would support his wife and vanquish their oppressors.*

Anything?

> *But the pressure of the moment has emptied his mind…*

Anything?

> *Ben shrugs, shakes his head. Nope.*
>
> *Alice is all out of answers. This party didn't work. Ben isn't up to it and perhaps she isn't either?*
>
> *They've lost.*

So…

> *She looks at her watch.*

This has been so fun.

DANNY. It really has been.

ALICE. I was about to look at my watch and was like, "Wait, how did it get this late that quickly?"

> *Ben sees the angle she's playing and joins in.*

BEN. I was just having the same—

ALICE. Crazy, right?

BEN. So crazy. The passage of time.

> *Pause.*
>
> *Ben and Alice wait to see if their guests will take the hint. Then—*

DORIS. We should probably get going.

> *Immediate protestations from Ben and Alice as everyone gets to their feet to say their overlapping goodbyes.*

ALICE. *(Overlapping.)* What?

BEN. *(Overlapping.)* No!

ALICE. *(Overlapping.)* I wasn't saying! I didn't mean!

DORIS. *(Overlapping.)* No, no, it's getting late.

BEN. *(Overlapping.)* I just put my party shoes on.

DANNY. *(Overlapping.)* Haha. Doris is right.

ALICE. *(Overlapping.)* Now I feel bad about bringing up the time.

DORIS. *(Overlapping.)* You shouldn't, Alice, that's silly.

BEN. *(Overlapping.)* Can't believe this.

DANNY. *(Overlapping.)* Quit while we're ahead.

BEN. *(Overlapping.)* Alice, are we really going to let them?

ALICE. *(Overlapping.)* I know.

DORIS. *(Overlapping.)* It's fine. And besides Danny has.

DANNY. *(Overlapping.)* I gotta go by and check on something.

DORIS. *(Overlapping.)* We've had such a lovely time.

BEN. *(Overlapping.)* This is crazy! We won't allow it!

DANNY. *(Overlapping.)* Aw, that's so sweet. He's threatening us.

ALICE. *(Overlapping.)* Haha. Right? He's putting his foot down.

BEN. *(Overlapping.)* I really am. I'm putting my foot right down onto the floor.

DORIS. *(Overlapping.)* Okay, then.

> *Throwing up his hands and crossing to the downstage door.*

BEN. *(Overlapping.)* Alright, alright. We tried.

DORIS. *(Cutting through.)* Ben. You convinced us. You win.

> *A confused beat.*

BEN. Win what? What did I win?

DORIS. If you won't allow it. We'll stay.

> *Doris sits back down on the couch. Danny joins her.*

BEN. *(Blurts out.)* NO!

DORIS. *(To Alice.)* For one more song.

BEN. No, no, no, no. That's not what I meant.

> *Alice gets it. She sits on the couch across from them. Trying to read this new turn of events—*

ALICE. One more song?

BEN. That isn't what I meant!

ALICE. *(To Ben.)* Hold on, sweetheart.

> *Ben begins to pace, his panic growing.*

BEN. I was saying if they gotta go, they gotta go.

ALICE. And then that's it?

DORIS. Then we really do have to go.

BEN. I thought Danny had to go check on something?

DANNY. It can wait.

BEN. Wait, wait. This is crazy.

ALICE. Sweetheart—

BEN. I didn't mean "not allow" as in they should stay.

ALICE. It's okay. I know what they want.

BEN. What?

ALICE. It's okay.

BEN. Now I'm the one who feels bad because I *really* REALLY *did not mean—*

ALICE. *(Cuts him off.)* Ben, stop. Just let me… *(Clocking Danny and Doris.)* So, you're saying…?

BEN. Not the Cat Stevens.

ALICE. I know that, Ben.

> *Her mind turning, Alice glances back at Ben and then returns to the guests. Decision made, she rises.*

Maybe we'll surprise you.

> *Alice exits. Anticipating, Ben extends a hand to stop Danny.*

BEN. She's got it.

> *Ben is lost, abandoned trying to make sense of this development.*

(Half question, half statement.) One more song. *(Then.)* So curious what she chooses.

DANNY. *(Agrees.)* Um-hm.

> *Beat.*

> *A song like Tears for Fears's "Shout" suddenly comes loud over the speakers.*[*]

BEN. *(Stands, startled.)* Hey!

> *The song cuts out after one or two seconds.*

ALICE. *(Offstage.)* Sorry!

BEN. Breaking our eardrums out here!

ALICE. *(Offstage.)* Not that one! Sorry!

BEN. It's okay, sweetheart! *(Referring to Alice.)* Not exactly great with technology.

DANNY. Aw. Poor thing.

> *Danny sets down his wine.*

BEN. She's okay though. She's got it.

DANNY. I know.

> *Danny stands and crosses stage right.*

BEN. *(Putting his foot down.)* No, no, NO, NO!

> *Danny stops.*

(Imploring.) HOW DARE YOU?!

> *Danny finally responds.*

DANNY. Or what? *(Then.)* Hold it? Or do I pee in the plant?

BEN. O-oh, you're—?

DANNY. Going to the bathroom. If I may?

BEN. 'Course. Sorry.

> *Danny crosses to the bathroom and exits stage left.*

> *Rattled, Ben returns to sit.*

> *Ben is left alone with Doris for the first time.*

(Referring to Danny, making fun of himself.) I thought he was going to, you know…

> *He gestures.*

…lie on top of her.

Doris doesn't respond.

(Waving her away, muttering.) Who cares?

    Ben can't even look at her so he feigns interest in the coffee table.

(Musing nonsense.) Celery celery celery…sticks.

    Like before, Ben begins to bob his head and murmur the lyrics to the earlier hip-hop song he sang to himself—

    Doris puts an end to that—

DORIS. You have something on your sleeve.

    Ben looks at a stain on his jacket sleeve as if it were emblematic of some universal meaninglessness.

BEN. *(Flatly croaking.)* Ranch.

    Once again, Doris does that strange "gag."

    Ben looks at her.

That isn't real.

DORIS. Yes, it is.

BEN. No, no, you're just. *(Then.)* You didn't really break that kid's arm.

    Doris patiently draws out his answer with a benevolent calm.

DORIS. Why would I say something like that if it wasn't true?

BEN. To scare us.

DORIS. Why would I want to do that?

BEN. …I don't know.

DORIS. Yes, you do.

BEN. *(Fear and desperation building and rising.)* No, I don't! I don't! I don't know anything! I mean I know I love Alice, I know that. I know she loves me, mostly. I know that my job is pointless and boring. I know that I don't have children. I know that Sunday is *Bernie Mac* and Monday is *Two and a Half Men.* Everything else is just me guessing! *(Then.)* I mean I suspect that not knowing how to make fire or dress a gunshot wound is going to come back and haunt me at some point, but I also think that I'm afraid all the time and that that could make me not see things clearly which would make me not know anything at all which is why I'm asking you.

DORIS. What are you asking *about*?

BEN. I'm asking about the arm! The arm! The toilet! The tennis courts! The lady in the coatroom! What the heck is going on out there?! There's Asian pythons in Florida now! You know that? Asian pythons in Florida up to fifteen feet long. Lives on dogs and toddlers all because someone couldn't afford frozen mice. I mean for heck's sake! I want to understand it but I don't. Was it always this bad and I didn't notice? Or is this something new? It feels worse now. Feels unfair, more mean, more dumb. Like somehow all of the bad people in the world got rich and interesting, while all of the good people lost their sense of humor and had to live in small apartments.

> *Ben's so caught up in his discussion with Doris, he doesn't notice Danny quietly emerge from the bathroom…*

But maybe I'm wrong about that? Maybe it's not that bad at all? Maybe it's all just a matter of perspective and I would feel better if I exercised and volunteered at a hospital, but before I do I just need to know how bad it is.

> *Danny walks calmly across the stage and disappears into the bedroom. Doris ignores this.*

That's my question, okay? That there, that is what I'm asking you. *How worried should I be?*

DORIS. I don't think you should be worried at all.

BEN. *(Snorts skeptically.)* Right, right. Just eat your snacks and watch your shows. Everything's gonna be just fine.

DORIS. No. That's not what I mean.

BEN. Okay, then. What do you mean?

DORIS. I mean worrying won't save you. Worrying's not the answer.

BEN. Okay, so. What's the answer?

> *Doris considers, as if perhaps reluctant to say.*

What is the answer? Tell me.

DORIS. You know.

> *Ben is filled with dread. He does know. But he needs to hear her say it.*

BEN. What is the answer?

DORIS. *(Simply.)* It's why we're here, isn't it? You invited us. You have to fight.

*A song like Duran Duran's "Rio" begins to play really loud.**
(We can barely hear the dialogue over it.)

BEN. *(Standing.)* Too loud! Too Loud!

Ben now notices the offstage bathroom door is open.

Danny?

Ben crosses to the bedroom door and looks in.

Something's happening in there.

(Screams.) ALICE!

The music continues to blare as Ben comes back center.

We can't hear him over the music, but he starts to rap to himself once again. But this time he's becoming galvanized as he runs through the defiant choreography—he's become music-video Cool J. Ready for action, Ben disappears into the bedroom.

The music cuts out. We hear the sound of violence. Exertion, men fighting, breathing heavily, shouting, maybe the sound of something shattering.

As this offstage life-and-death struggle continues, we start to build in those "outside world" noises again. The rumble of a train, a car horn, a lion's roar, the murmur of a teeming market, etc.

Onstage, Doris pulls off her heels and lets herself get comfortable. She eats a popper. Mmm. Maybe the taste is growing on her? She eats another and picks up the TV remote off the table. Doris studies it a moment, looking for the right button.

The "outside world" sounds grow louder and louder and louder, becoming a cacophony.

Doris points the remote at the downstage TV…

The sounds and lights go out.

End of Play